The Medie

THEN AND THERE SERIES
CREATED BY MARJORIE REEVES
GENERAL EDITOR: JOHN FINES

The Medieval Knight

MARJORIE REEVES

Illustrated from contemporary sources

Longman

LONGMAN GROUP UK LIMITED,
*Longman House, Burnt Mill, Harlow,
Essex CM20 2JE, England
and Asssociated Companies throughout the world.*

Published in the United States of America by Longman Inc., New York.

First published 1988

*Set in 11/13 point Rockwell Light (Linotron)
Printed in Great Britain
by Butler and Tanner Ltd, Frome*

ISBN 0 582 01461 1

For Tom Ainsworth

Contents

Acknowledgements

For permission to reproduce photographs we are grateful to the following: BBC Hulton Picture Library, pages 3, 10, 17, 34; Bodleian Library, Oxford, page 30; The British Library, pages 7, 9, 13, 15, 16, 19, 40, 43, 45, 47; Master & Fellows of Corpus Christy College, Cambridge, page 27; Mansell Collection, pages 2, 23; Pierpont Morgan Library, page 11 *below*; Walter Scott (Bradford), page 37; Victoria & Albert Museum, page 39.

COVER: An armed knight of Prato from a 14th century address by the people of Prato to their protector Robert of Anjou, King of Naples. MS Royal 6 E IX fol. 24. Photo: The British Library.

To the reader

Have you come across the word **chivalry** or heard someone say: 'He is very **chivalrous**'? Today we use these words to describe men who have polite manners and help other people, especially those weaker than themselves. But these words go right back to the days when knights rode around in armour on horseback. The word chivalry comes from the French word for a horse, *cheval*, and was first used to describe men who fought on horses. It is actually the same word as our word for horse soldiers, cavalry. But besides learning to fight on horses, medieval knights also learnt to obey a lot of special rules about how they should fight bravely, how they should behave politely to ladies and how they should serve their lords faithfully and never let them down. People called these the rules of chivalry and that is how the words get their modern meaning. They also talked about **courtesy** and being **courteous**. These words come from the court of the castles where knights and ladies lived. They also meant good manners and politeness. In medieval times knights were important soldiers. In this book you will read stories about how they fought and how they lived. They are no longer important today as fighting men, but we still use their words.

Words printed in **thick black** are explained in the Glossary on page 52.

Note: The extracts from source material in this book are freely translated and summarised from Latin and old French.

1 Growing up in a medieval castle

If you were the son or daughter of a baron in the time of King Henry II, you would probably not go to school. But you would learn all sorts of things in the castle in which you lived. It was not a comfortable home. The stone **keep** was cold and draughty and the wind blew all the way down the winding stone staircase from the **battlements**. But people were beginning to improve their castles and when you were little you would probably sleep with your father and mother in a separate room that might even have a fire-place.

In the great hall the soldiers doing castle-guard ate their meals and slept. Many of the knights holding lands round-about had the duty of sending so many soldiers in turn to **garrison** the castle for one or two months at a time. You would see them clattering up and down the stairways as they kept watch in turn on the castle walls.

A busy castle

Imagine yourself climbing up to that windy walk which runs all round the top of the keep and marching round with the guard who watch the countryside or the river to spy out everyone approaching the castle. Then you descend right down to ground level and go to see what the castle servants are doing at their various jobs in the inner or outer **bailey**. The grooms in the stables are currying the horses, the blacksmith at his forge is beating out a sword or perhaps

Here the blacksmith is hammering the handle (or pommel) of the sword into shape.

sharpening one, and the carpenter is making a bench for the hall or a cradle for a new baby.

The stonemason is repairing a weak place in the castle wall and the arrow-maker or **fletcher** is whittling away, piling up sheaves of arrows for the great longbows which he looks after so carefully. The lord's huntsmen may be out scouring the woods to see where the beasts lie; if not, they will be looking after their hounds, while the **falconers** are busy feeding the hooded hawks on their perches (carefully keeping their fingers away from those cruel beaks). On a special grass plot the washerwoman is spreading linen to dry and a cook is picking herbs for flavouring in the little herb garden.

As it is peacetime the gates lie open and the drawbridge over the moat is down. Trundling up the steep slope and rumbling over the bridge come the country carts full of things the castle folk need – meat, flour, barley, firewood, hay and so on. The peasants in the surrounding villages are mostly tenants of the lord and must work in the lord's fields and harvest his crops. Some may be bringing live sheep or hens to be kept till needed.

In the keep

Back in the keep, everyone is equally busy. The cooks are scurrying about in the kitchen, stirring the huge cauldron of stew, mixing sauces, pulling loaves out of the oven and shouting to the boy who turns the spit on which great joints of meat are roasting.

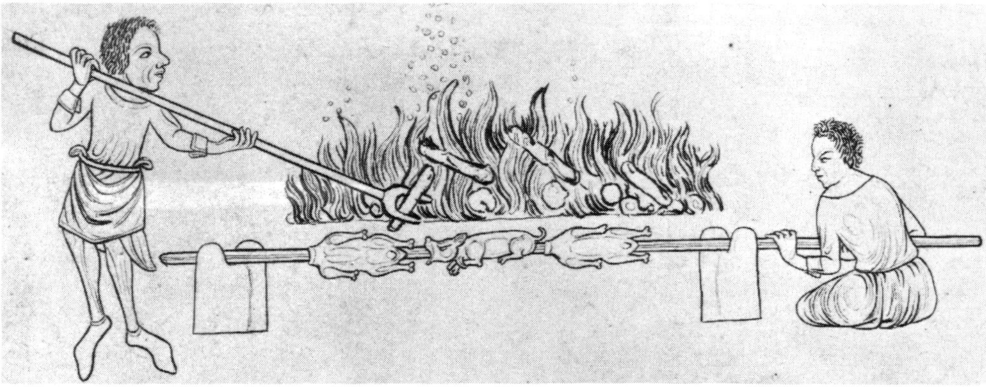

Roasting meat, a picture from the Luttrell Psalter. Which is the turnspit? What kind of meat is he roasting and why does he keep turning the spit round? What is the other person doing?

In the great hall servants are scrubbing the **pewter tankards** with sand and laying fresh rushes on the floor. In the little chapel the family chaplain has finished saying Mass and is carefully putting his **vestments** in their chest. The lady of the castle is in her bower with the sewing women. They must work hard, for they spin and weave the cloth as well as making the clothes for the castle people. In his own chamber the lord of the castle sits doing business with his **steward**. They go over accounts together, talk about good and bad tenants and discuss the castle defences. Then the steward gets ready to ride off to one of the lord's manors where he will hold a court for the lord and settle all the disputes. The lord has to govern a great many tenants and their affairs. If the castle is the centre of his **honour**, that is, of all his lands, he will sometimes hold an important court in the castle for all his tenants.

This is only an imaginary picture of what you would find going on, but it shows you the most important things that had to be attended to if you lived in a castle. Garrison, armour and weapons, food supplies, strong walls – these were the first things the lord had to think about. But there were other things in life as well: governing your people well, teaching your sons to be good knights, hunting and sporting, feasting and making music, worshipping God and making yourself ready for the sudden death that might come at any time. Every good lord tried to leave to his children more lands than he had inherited and he would share them out carefully in his will.

Learning to be a page-boy

It was exciting to be a boy living in a great castle. When you had grown up a bit your father would probably send you to be educated in the household of some other great lord. First you would learn to be a page. The main duty of a page was to serve his lord at meals. This part of his education had a lot to do with good manners. Someone wrote a book telling small pages how to behave. He called them 'babies' and this is some of what he said:

> Fair Babies, when you enter your lord's place say 'God speed' and salute all there. Hold up your head and kneel on one knee to your lord. If any speak to you, look straight at them and listen well. Stand till you are told to sit down, keep your hands and feet quiet and don't scratch yourself. Bow to your lord when you answer him. Be always ready to serve at the proper time, to bring drink, hold lights or anything else. When your lord is ready for dinner, pour out water and hold the towel till he has finished. Stand by your lord till he tells you to sit. Cut your bread, don't break it. Don't lean on the table or dirty the cloth, or hang your head over your dish or eat with a full mouth. Don't dip your meat in the salt-cellar or put your knife

in your mouth or make a noise eating. When the meal is over, clean your knives and put them in their places, rise without laughing and joking and go to your lord's table and stand there till grace is said.

How the girls were educated

Girls, like their brothers, were often sent to be educated in a large household. There the lady of the castle could teach them many things. They would sit in her bower learning to spin and weave and perhaps embroider exciting pictures of stories in bright colours to hang on the walls. The lady would show them how to make medicines out of herbs and marzipan sweetmeats in the shape of ships or castles or animals. Perhaps they did not have such an interesting time as their brothers, but, as you will see, there were lively shows to watch and sometimes they had adventures.

Things to do

1. What was the work of the castle guard, the grooms, the blacksmith, the fletcher, the falconer, the chaplain and the steward? You could draw pictures to illustrate.
2. Read the instructions to page-boys carefully on pages 4 and 5. What do they tell us about some people's bad manners?
3. Would you have liked to be a page-boy or a girl living in a medieval castle? Give reasons for your answers.

2 Learning to be a squire and knight

A squire's duties

In their teens boys became 'squires' and began the warlike part of their education. You would probably become the squire of one particular lord. You would learn to keep his armour polished and ready for use and to dress him in it correctly. You saw to his horses and when he went to a **tournament** or on a war expedition you accompanied him. You were not allowed to fight yourself but one of your special duties was to lead and guard your lord's baggage-horses. In a tournament your part was rather like that of a second in a boxing match: you would look after your lord when he came out of the fray and take bits of battered armour to be repaired for next day.

All the time you would be watching and learning about how a knight fought. You would learn how to put on armour and carry its weight, how to balance your **lance** on horseback and how to use your sword.

Fighting on horseback was tricky because it was very easy to fall off when fighting another knight. So all the squires practised hard riding at the **quintain**. This was a stand with two revolving arms on which hung a shield and a sandbag. The game was to ride up at the gallop, strike the shield with your lance, and then wheel your horse out of the way before the sandbag swung round and hit you. In a real battle, of course, it would be your opponent's weapon that you would have to avoid, not a sandbag.

You would do this practise in a flat open space called a **tilting yard**. There was also sword practice to do and **archery** practice, that is, learning to shoot your arrows

Above: Riding at the quintain. Is he going to hit the shield? This picture is from a thirteenth-century book.

dead on to the targets, called the **butts**. A squire had a lot to learn. He would ride at the quintain until he had got the trick perfectly. But so long as he was a squire he had to keep in the background. If he tried to get in the front battle line he was ordered back severely.

Besides learning to fight you had to learn how to behave in polite society, especially among the ladies. This meant learning to carve neatly at dinner, to dance elegantly and to sing and perhaps play a musical instrument. It was pleasant entertaining the ladies and quite often a squire would fall in love with one of the girls.

A story about a love-sick squire

This story is told by a **troubadour** (a songwriter):

> Fairer and fairer still than I can say was Blonde, the earl of Oxford's daughter. She sat at dinner and was served by Jehan the squire, fair and free of body, who pained himself much to earn all men's graces by his courteous service. He waited not on his lady alone, but up and down the hall, knight and lady, squire and page, groom and messenger, all he served according to their desire and thus from all he earned goodwill.
>
> After dinner they washed their hands and went to play, each as he would, up in the forest or down by

the river, in some sort of pastime. Jehan oftentimes would go to play in the Countess's bower. Well he knew all chamber games – chess and backgammon and dice – whereas he **diverted** the lady Blanche (the countess).

One day, as Blonde sat at table, it was for Jehan to carve before her. By chance he cast his eyes on her; yet he had seen her daily these eighteen weeks past. From this look such thoughts came into his head that on his carving he thought no more. Blonde who marked his thoughts astray, took upon her to rebuke him and bade him think of his carving without delay. Seeing that Jehan heard her not, then spake she again: 'Carve, Jehan! Are you sleeping or dreaming here? I pray you give me now to eat; of your courtesy, dream no more'. At this word Jehan heard her voice; therewith he started as one who is shaken suddenly from his sleep. He seized the knife as a man in a dream and thought to carve well and fair, but so distraught was he that he cut deep into two fingers; forth sprang the blood as he rose from table and sad was Blonde at that sight. Jehan prayed another squire to carve before his lady and went forthwith to his own chamber.

Becoming a knight

Of course every squire looked forward eagerly to the day when his education would be over and he would be knighted. This might happen suddenly on a battlefield but often it was a solemn ceremony planned beforehand. The young man would take a bath, put on fresh clothes and a beautiful new cloak and kneel before the one who was to knight him. This lord would dub him a knight by striking him on the shoulder with his sword and then gird on his sword-belt and sword. The great thing was to be knighted by an important prince or lord whom you admired very much.

These men are being knighted. What exactly is happening? This picture comes from a medieval book of stories about knights.

The armoury

Now the new knight would get full armour. This was kept in a part of the castle keep called the **armoury** and the **armourer** – a very important person – was in charge of it. It was the armourer's job to inspect all the armour and weapons regularly and give the blacksmith his orders. Weak links in **chain mail** must be repaired at once lest a sword or lance thrust or an arrow might pierce through. Dents must be hammered out of helmets, swords sharpened and lances inspected, for if the **shaft** was weak it might splinter to bits at the first thrust. Besides the equipment for knights, the archers' longbows had to be always ready, unstrung until needed because this kept the spring in the wood, but with the bowstrings always well greased. Sheaves of arrows were ready, the battle-axes, spears and long knives for the foot-soldiers. For armour these men usually wore padded leather tunics and helmets.

Putting on your armour

If you went to watch the new knight arming himself you would see that first he put on a **hauberk**, that is, a shirt made of tiny linked rings of iron (chain mail). Some knights wore a padded leather tunic, called **gambeson**, under this shirt of mail. Then probably your knight would protect his legs with coverings of chain mail called **chausses**. He

Two famous knights in full armour as we can still see them carved on their tombs. Which are the hauberk, chausses and surcoat? Fashions in helmets changed but both these could be closed over the face.

would gird on his sword-belt and sword and finally put on his helmet.

In the armoury there were many of these helmets hanging up. Some were old-fashioned ones – the sort men wore at the Battle of Hastings about a hundred years before. These were **conical** in shape, with no covering for the face except a nose-piece. But the newest fashion in helmets was a large, flat-topped one which covered the whole head. All the younger knights would want to be up-to-date in their helmets. These new ones protected your face but they had two disadvantages – they were heavy to wear and no one could see who you were. So, in battle, knights were just beginning to wear badges on their shields and on top of their helmets so that their friends would not mistake them for enemies. A little later these become the family badges we call **coats of arms** but in the twelfth century they were just personal badges chosen by each knight. Some knights put on a sleeveless linen tunic, called a **surcoat**, over their hauberks and they often had their badges embroidered on these. This is why we speak of a coat of arms.

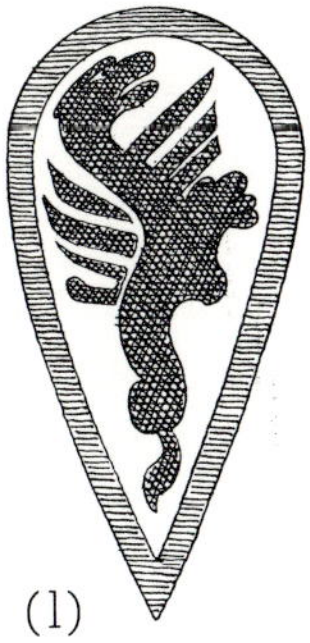

(1)

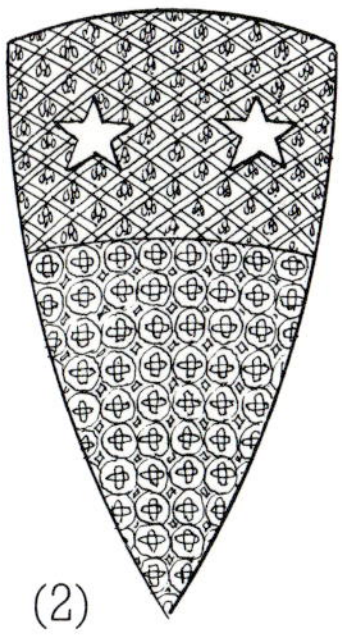

(2)

There was fashions in shields as well as helmets. You could tell if a knight was using his father's shield because it would be shaped like a long kite, as in picture (1), while the newer ones were like picture (2).

Now, with sword, helmet and shield complete, your knight only needed to pick up a good stout lance from the armoury and he would be ready for fighting. But although this armour is not as heavy as it will be two centuries later, it is still heavy enough, especially for a young, new knight. So if he has only been dressing up to show you he will be anxious to get it off. This thirteenth-century drawing shows what it was like getting out of a hauberk.

A knight's excuses for fighting

Fighting was natural to these knights and they could hardly stop themselves doing it. But they knew that warfare was brutal, so they wanted to have a good excuse for it – a good cause to fight for. One good reason was loyalty. Knights took **oaths of fealty** or faithfulness to their lords and if the lord summoned his **vassal** to fight, the knight's duty was to support him through thick and thin, whatever the cause of the war might be.

Knights also believed that it was right to fight in defence of the old and the weak, and especially ladies. But I am afraid that these knights did not think much about protecting poor, defenceless peasants.

Thirdly, every good knight wished to fight for God. This usually meant fighting the heathen Saracens who were conquering Palestine and advancing along the Mediterranean as far as Spain. It was a great heroic adventure for a knight to take the vow of a **crusader** and go off to fight in far and strange places. He might be captured and spend years as a slave, he might never return, but he believed that he was using his skill to fight for God.

Things to do

1. Draw a picture of a quintain to show how it worked.
2. Write the story of Jehan as if told by Blonde.
3. Draw a knight in full armour and name the parts of his armour.
4. Has your school got a coat of arms? If so, how old is it and what does it mean? If you can find some old coats of arms, draw them and find out the proper names for the different parts from a book on heraldry.

3 Tournaments, hunting and feasts

Spring was the time when knights began to polish up their armour and think about fighting. One famous troubadour sang a spring song, not about bright flowers and birds singing but about going to war. Here is a bit of it:

> Spring is the time when knights go out to war, when the meadows are white with **pavilions**, when shepherds and their flocks scurry away from the advance-guards of armies, when the earth trembles beneath the hooves of chargers, when castles are **beleaguered** and walls and towers crumble down in ruins.

Knights at a tournament

Can you tell which of the knights below is going to win this round in the tournament? This picture comes from the Luttrell Psalter.

But if there was no war on, summer was the time for tournaments, that is, mock fights for practice. When a tournament was announced at a castle, knights would come riding in from miles around to take part. There were very strict rules for fighting and these would be announced by

a herald with a trumpet. One particular lord would be appointed as umpire and judge. The tournament would be held on flat, open ground, perhaps in the tilting yard and all around there would be pavilions for the competing knights and stands for the spectators, with bright flags fluttering from them. The stands where the ladies sat were the most colourful and perhaps there would be a chief lady, a queen or a countess, who sat in a special stand and presented prizes at the end.

The first round of the tournament was between two knights with lances on horseback. They galloped towards each other from opposite ends of the field. Each aimed at knocking his opponent off his horse with a heavy blow from his lance. The best way of getting real power behind this blow was to strike when your horse was moving at his fastest speed. So they thundered towards each other and everyone held their breath. If one succeeded in unhorsing the other at the first charge, that was the end of that round in the fight. But sometimes they both missed and had to gallop on until they could turn their horses and come back for a second attack. Sometimes they both kept their seats, thrusting at each other with heavy blows, as they hit and galloped and wheeled round to come in again. The fight went on until finally one was unhorsed, unless one of them was badly injured when the umpire would throw down his baton and end the fight.

The second round

The second round would be on foot with swords. They would thrust at each other fiercely and hard blows would ring on iron helmets. But the aim was not to kill but to force your opponent to his knees or strike his sword out of his hand. Contests like this went on all day between different pairs of knights. And sometimes there were mock battles when whole groups of knights fought each other. Sometimes there were accidents when a knight got badly injured or even killed, but what the knights really aimed at was skill in disarming or unhorsing their opponents, not hurting them. The audience applauded loudly when a knight was specially skilful and many of the knights fought to win the ladies' applause.

The ladies watched intently, for they all had their favourites. Often a knight had a special lady-love and she would give him a glove or a scarf to wear as a **favour** in a tournament. So while the tournament was going on she would be watching for the knight with, say, her scarf twisted round his helmet and hoping he would win. If he won a prize he thought of it as an honour to his lady. Knights did not often marry these ladies. Marriage was rather a business matter: you must marry a girl with lands who would make you richer. Often these marriages were quite happy ones, but all the same a young knight enjoyed paying honour to his beautiful lady-love.

Sports

Besides tournaments there were plenty of good sports, especially hawking and hunting. When the countryside was peaceful, the lord, with his knights, would ride out merrily across the drawbridge when the first sunbeams were beginning to sparkle on the trees to go hawking. The powerful hawks or **falcons** would be perched, bound and

A hawking party which was drawn in Queen Mary's Psalter in the early fourteenth century. What do you think the man is saying to the lady? What is the boy doing?

hooded, on their wrists, apparently fast asleep. Suddenly, with a whirr of wings, the party would rouse up the birds they were after – quails, cranes, wild geese and so on. Then quickly one of the hawkers would slip off the hood and leather strap binding the hawk. Instantly he would come to life, mounting up and up into the blue sky above his **quarry**, and swooping suddenly and terribly to strike down the poor bird with his cruel beak. Each sportsman had his own hawk and they would play one against the other to see which was the best.

Hunting

They might take the dogs to go hunting the hare or the fox or in wintertime there might be an exciting boar hunt. This could be dangerous, for wild **boars** had sharp tusks and might charge at the huntsmen when angry. Above all, knights loved to hunt the shy wild deer through the deep forest, but no lord could hunt just where and what he pleased. There were large stretches of country called royal forests where no one could hunt unless the king gave him permission.

King Henry II himself loved hunting. If you were a huntsman in a royal castle you would be busy all the time, tracking down the deer, keeping the horses and hounds in good shape, preparing for the next time the king came.

This hunting picture also comes from Queen Mary's Psalter. Why do you think the huntsman is blowing his horn?

Then, perhaps late one night, the king would come riding in from a distant castle. He would throw himself down to sleep but you would have to be ready to be up and off at dawn to the green wood with him. He would hunt furiously, come back to the castle, hold a solemn council on important government business, feast long, sleep a little, and be up again by sunrise to ride to the next castle. Henry II was a restless, energetic king.

Indoor games

There were plenty of indoor games for stormy winter days. They played chess, backgammon and dice. Even grownups enjoyed what we call children's games and the great hall was a fine place for a game of blindman's buff or battledore and shuttlecock. They danced merrily, sometimes in a circle, sometimes in a long line, to the music of pipe and drum or a very early kind of fiddle.

The game of Hoodman Blind in which one player puts his hood over his face and then has to guess who has hit him with a hood. Why do the other players knot their hoods?

There is a **contemporary** story about two brothers who were playing dice in the **solar** above the hall. They were bored so they began to make a terrific noise and when a third brother tried to stop them, they started to pour water on him down the stairs. He rushed into the hall with his sword drawn shouting to them to fight. Only their father was able to stop the fight but this quarrel started a feud between the brothers which went on for years. This shows what could happen if the castle garrison got bored.

Feasting

Feasting came late in the day, after the tournaments or hunts were over. Nobody ate much breakfast: a hunk of bread or a drink of ale was probably enough as you went off to your work or your sport. Again, lunch was light, if you had any at all. Dinner was the thing – in the afternoon or evening. Work was done so now you could enjoy yourself and most people could eat a lot more at once than we can. It was all done with great ceremony. The torches round the walls of the great hall would be flaring in their **sconces**, the fire would blaze and the lord would seat himself in his great chair at the high table. Beside him would be his lady wife and his children. Guests and chief knights would also be seated at the high table. Everyone else had his proper place at the long wooden tables which stretched down the length of the hall.

First, the pages would carry bowls of water and napkins to the high table for everyone to wash and dry their hands. Then from the doors at the far end of the hall would come a procession of serving men with great steaming dishes and, if it was a great feast, the procession would be led by trumpets. The first dishes would be carried up to the high table and there the pages and squires would carve the meat and serve the diners on bended knee. They would pour wine into the silver drinking goblets and bring basins of water and napkins again at the end of the meal, for there were no forks and the diners used their fingers. The rest of the company did not dine so elegantly: they picked the meat off the bones with their teeth and drank out of pewter tankards.

Above: A drawing of a feast from a fourteenth-century book. Find the musicians. What is happening on the right and left-hand sides of the picture?

The meal went on for a long time as you can guess from this sample menu:

Boar's head with its tusks decorated with flowers. Venison, cranes, peacocks, swans, kids, pigs, hens. Spiced and seasoned meats with red and white wine in great plenty. Pheasants, woodcock, partridges, larks and plovers, well-roasted with brawn and other things. White powder (blanc-mange) and large sweets.

Entertainment

After dinner, especially in the dark winter evenings, knights and ladies liked to listen to songs about love and war. Some of these were long story poems called **ballads** about great deeds in battle or adventures of knights. The latest fashion in the time of King Henry II were stories about King Arthur and his knights. The real Arthur had lived hundreds of years before this, but people in the twelfth century were making up stories about his adventures. They liked to imagine Arthur and his knights dressed in the same kind of armour as themselves and riding to the same sort of tournament or battle as they did themselves.

Some of these story poems were about people actually living in the twelfth century. There is a long one called 'The Romance of the FitzWarines' all about a famous family. In it there is a boy called Fulk. Now here is a story from this poem.

The story of Fulk FitzWarine in Ludlow Castle

When Fulk was seven he was sent to be educated in the household of Joce de Dinan, Lord of Ludlow Castle. It was an exciting life because Joce had a feud with his neighbour, Hugh de Lacy. One morning, when Fulk was about seventeen, they looked out from a tower at Ludlow and saw the meadows gleaming with spears: de Lacy's men were riding towards the castle! Hastily Joce gathered his knights together – about 500 of them – and charged out of the gate. They attacked so fiercely that de Lacy's men turned tail in flight. Joce saw de Lacy riding away alone and, galloping after him, was just going to take him prisoner, when three of de Lacy's men dashed up and attacked Joce. On the castle wall Joce's wife and two daughters Sybil and Hawyse, had been anxiously watching the fight. When they saw Joce attacked by three men they shrieked out loudly. Young Fulk had been left behind in the castle but now the Lady Hawyse taunted him with remaining safe while her father was in danger of his life. So Fulk, stung by her scorn, rushed out of the castle to Joce's rescue. He and Joce together fought so well that they killed two of the enemy and brought back a knight named Arnold as a prisoner.

This part of the story ended happily, for the Lady Hawyse praised Fulk's bravery and in the end married him. But there is another piece of the story about the prisoner, Arnold. A beautiful girl in the castle, named Marion, fell in love with Arnold who persuaded her to help him escape. So one dark night she made a rope from pieces of linen and he slid down the castle wall from a window and escaped. Fulk and the Lady Hawyse had a splendid wedding and after it Joce de Dinan and most of his household rode away on a visit, leaving a very small garrison behind. But Marion pretended to be ill and stayed behind as well. She sent a secret message to her lover, Arnold, telling him that Ludlow was held by only a few knights. So de Lacy and Arnold planned to surprise the castle. On a moonless night, Arnold, with a hundred men, crept up under the castle wall. There Marion was waiting at a window to drop down a cord. Arnold fastened a leather ladder to this which she drew up. While the garrison were sleeping, Arnold and his men slipped up the ladder, killed the guard and captured the castle. But in the morning Marion was filled with remorse because she had been a traitor. So she seized her lover's sword, killed him as he slept and then flung herself to death from a window. As for Fulk, he and the Lady Hawyse went to the court of King Henry where they became rich and famous.

Things to do

1. In any good game there is a set of rules. Read the account of the way knights fought in a tournament (pages 14 and 15) and then draw up a set of rules for fair play in a tournament.
2. You are a lady watching a tournament. Write a story about your favourite knight and the way he fights.
3. Paint a picture of feasting in the great hall. The picture on page 19 will help you.
4. How many different words can you find for hawk? Use your dictionary. Find out what all the different birds in the dinner menu on page 19 look like.
5. Make up a troubadour song about springtime.

4 The story of William the Marshal (part 1)

There was one famous knight whom everyone knew about and after his death one of his followers wrote all his deeds in a long poem. The story of William the Marshal told here comes from that poem.

A small boy's adventure

His adventures began when he was about five or six years old. His father was called John the Marshal. He was fighting King Stephen (the king before Henry II) and one day, when the king was besieging one of his castles, he asked for a **truce**. This meant that he had to promise not to get food secretly into the castle while the truce lasted. To show that he would keep his promise, John had to give his fourth son William as a **hostage** to the king. So the little boy was taken as a prisoner to the king's camp. But his father had no intention of keeping his promise. He cruelly said that he had more sons and one did not matter so much to him as saving his castle. So he got food and more soldiers into his castle while the truce was on.

When King Stephen discovered that he had been tricked he was angry. By the rules of war he had the right to kill his child hostage in revenge. So Stephen's lords seized the boy to kill him. William did not understand what was happening at all. The poem tells the story of what happened next:

> As the boy was being led along, not dreaming he was going to his death, he saw the Earl of Arundel holding a very fine hunting-spear and he said innocently: 'Sire,

A mangonel for hurling stones at castle walls. Can you see where the stone was put and how the sling was released?

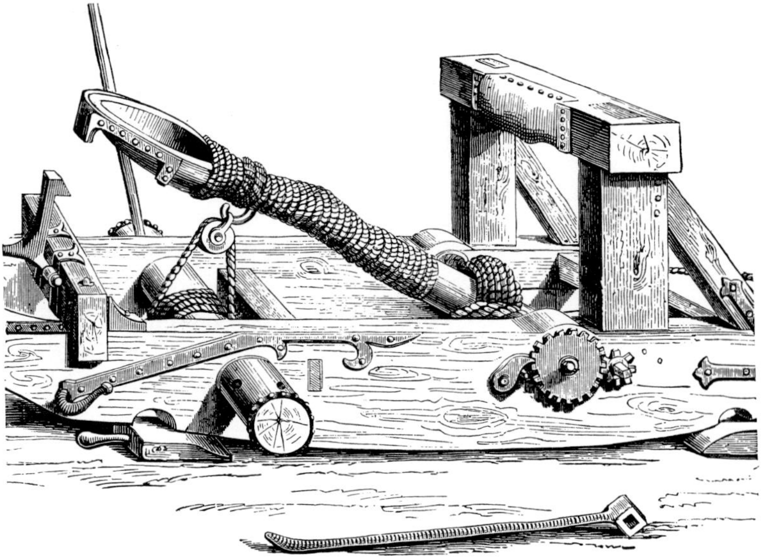

give me that spear!' When the king heard this childish remark, he would not allow him to be hanged that day, no, not for all the gold in France, but he took the boy in his arms and said: 'You are **reprieved** from this agonizing death; of a truth you shall not die today'.

They returned to the army and found the **mangonel** being got ready for hurling stones into the castle. Then some of the king's lords advised the king to take the boy straightaway, place him in the sling of the magonel and have him flung at the castle wall to strike terror into the defenders. The boy, little suspecting, was led up to the mangonel; he saw the sling and exclaimed:

'Goodness! What a big seesaw! Do let me have a go at it!' The king said: 'Let be! Let be! It would be wicked indeed to let him die in torment. His childish sayings are so pretty. Collect stones for the siege engine as heavy as you can manage.'

Some then worked the mangonel, while others made screens of hurdles to cover themselves as they attacked the gate. One of the ruffians dragged

William out in front of the castle and called out to the defenders. 'Here is the son of your lord and we are going to place him on top of the hurdles when we attack.' But they replied from the castle: 'Then he is doomed, for we shall squash him as flat as a pancake!' Then they hung a great millstone from the battlements, ready to drop on the hurdle-screens when they attacked. William asked what new kind of game they were hanging out of the window. The king laughed heartily and said: 'William, that game would not be good for you! Playthings such as that shall never be given to you. You shall never die by my command!'

William and King Stephen play 'knights'

So King Stephen saved William, but he kept the boy as a hostage for many weeks. William was quite at home in the camp. He played games with the soldiers and sometimes even with the king. One of the games he played with the king was rather like playing with conkers, only it was played with the long stalks and heads of plantains. Each player tries to strike off the head of the other player's plantain or 'knight'. This is the story of how William played 'knights' with King Stephen.

The king was resting one day during the siege. He was sitting in his tent which was strewn with grass and flowers of many colours. William went up and down looking at them. Eagerly and happily he set about picking up the 'knights'. When he had gathered enough in his fist, he said to the king: 'Fair and dear lord, would you like a game of knights?' 'Yes, indeed, fair, sweet friend,' replied the other. 'Which of us shall strike first?' said William. 'You', said the king, 'my fair and honoured friend.' So William took one of his knights and the king held out one of his and the result of this encounter was that the king's knight lost its head, to the great delight of William. The king held out another to him. But at this moment the boy saw through a slit in the tent one of his own mother's serving men. He had crept into the camp to spy out what was happening to William, for his mother was afraid of the hurt that might be done to him. William was overjoyed to see him and called out: 'Welcome, friend Willikin! Tell me who sent you hither! How is my lady-mother and my sisters and brothers?' The man slunk back out of sight and took to his heels rapidly up the narrow cart-track. The king heard William's cry of delight and asked him to whom he was speaking. He said: 'By the faith I owe my father, he was one of my mother's servants; he looked at me through that chink yonder.' Then they searched for him but he could not be found anywhere.

William becomes squire and knight

Lady Sibille, William's mother, must have been glad when her servant brought back good news. After a while William was returned to her safe and sound. When he was about thirteen, he was sent off across the sea to the Castle of Tancarville in Normandy, where his father's cousin, William, Lord of Tancarville, promised to educate him. There he learnt all the proper things and became a good squire to his lord. He had a huge appetite, he sang troubadour songs of love and war, and he said very little. He was very handsome and tall, and he was a favourite with his lord.

But for a long time he remained a squire, attending his lord at tournaments and in battle, looking after his horses and his armour, guarding his prisoners, but never allowed to win glory for himself in battle. At last, in 1167, when the Lord of Tancarville was fighting for his king, Henry II, he thought the time had come to knight William. So there and then, in the war-camp and therefore without much ceremony, William Marshal, dressed in a new cloak, was dubbed knight by his lord and girded with his sword.

William loses one horse and gets another

The first time William fought in a battle he was so anxious to be in front that he dashed forward and had to be called back to let more experienced knights lead the charge. All the same, he soon managed to get in front again. A Flemish soldier caught his shoulder with a great iron hook and dragged him off his horse in the midst of the enemy. William managed to get free of the hook and cut his way back to safety but he had lost his horse.

This was serious, for William was poor and could not afford another expensive war-horse. He sold the rich cloak in which he had been knighted and scraped up enough money to buy a baggage-horse to carry his armour. But when news came of a great tournament to be held at Le Mans (in France), William was sad, when everyone else was full of glee, because he could not ride into a tournament on an old baggage-horse. Finally, however, his lord gave him a splendid new war-horse, fast and strong. With the other young men of the castle William spent a busy night polishing his armour and weapons and at daybreak they all rode happily away.

The tournament was a big one in which forty knights fought at the same time on each side. William was determined to get a horse for himself. He rushed at a knight, captured him and made him promise to pay a **ransom**. Then he went back and captured two more knights. Altogether he did very well for himself: he gained fame as a good fighter and he got lots of booty – war-horses, baggage-horses, **palfreys** and armour.

Another tournament

William decided that he liked going to tournaments. He asked permission to go to another. In the first onslaught he handled his lance so skilfully that he unhorsed one of his opponents, but before he could capture him he was attacked by five other knights. He drew his sword and

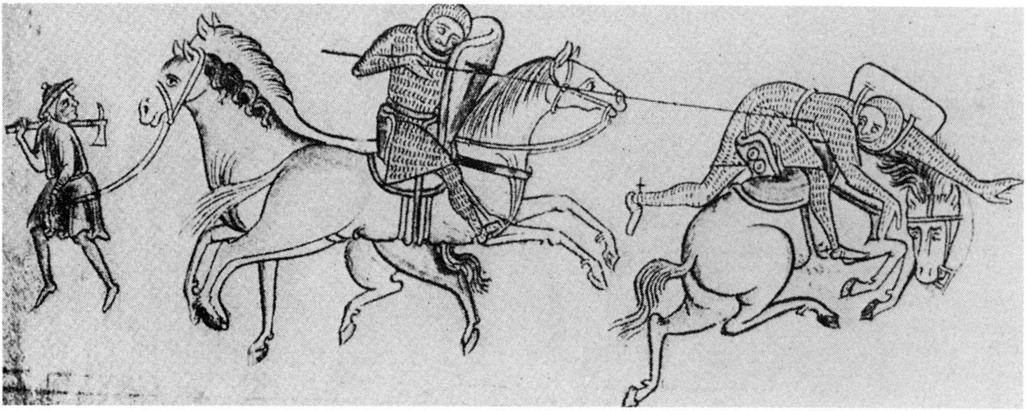

Unhorsing your opponent in a joust. This picture is from a thirteenth-century book.

smote all round him, but one of his opponents hit a great blow at his helmet which turned it right round back to front, so that William could hardly breathe. He had to retire to his tent to get it off. While he was standing inside, two well-known knights rode past. 'Sir John', said one, 'who is that knight so clever with his weapons?' 'That is William Marshal', said the other. 'There is no man more true.' William was so pleased to overhear these words that he got his helmet on again the right way, rode into the tournament once more and fought so well that he won the prize – another fine war-horse.

Ambush and danger

But life was not all tournaments. Once with his uncle, Earl Patrick, William was at Lusignan (in France) guarding Queen Eleanor, the wife of Henry II. One day, riding outside the castle, without their armour on, the queen, the earl and William were ambushed and attacked. The earl sent the queen galloping back to safety but before he could arm himself the earl was killed. Young William was hastily sliding into his hauberk when he saw his uncle fall. He was so angry at this treacherous attack that he vaulted on to his horse and charged the enemy without waiting to put on his helmet. The first man he met he cut down with a single sword-stroke. But the next man killed his horse. William quickly disentangled himself and placed his back against a hedge to fight it out single-handed. He kept it up for some time but at last a knight crept up the back of the hedge and leaning over it, thrust his sword into William's thigh.

So William was captured, bound, put on a horse and hurried away by his captors because they feared King Henry's vengeance. No one bound up his wound and he suffered much as they hustled him along. One night, when they were resting in a castle, a lady noticed that the prisoner was wounded. She cut the centre out of a loaf, filled it with bandages and sent the loaf to William. So he was able to bind up his wound properly and gradually it healed. At last Queen Eleanor, who was grateful to the young knight for fighting so fiercely, paid his ransom and gave him a rich reward of armour, horses and splendid clothes, as well as her favour.

William becomes tutor to the king's son, the young Henry

King Henry and Queen Eleanor thought so well of William Marshal that they made him tutor to their eldest son. William had to teach him to handle his lance and sword, to train him as a good knight and to guard him in tournament and battle. He was the captain of the young Henry's company of household knights. William won his young master's favour so much that when the time came for the prince to be knighted, he chose William Marshal to gird on his sword and dub him knight.

They had some narrow escapes together. One day in a fight the young Henry and William got separated from the rest of their knights and found themselves having to charge 300 foot-soldiers all by themselves. The soldiers were afraid of the galloping horses and let them through. But as they were thundering through, William seized the reins of the leader's horse (for he alone was mounted), capturing him right under the nose of his soldiers! They rode swiftly towards their own camp, but, as they went, a low-hanging branch swept the captive Frenchman right off his horse. William was in front, leading the horse, and had no idea that he had lost his prisoner. Henry, following, saw it all, but said nothing. When they reached the camp, William turned round in triumph to his prisoner and behold! he had only a riderless horse. Everyone roared with laughter when they saw his face.

More tournaments

William still enjoyed going to tournaments and sometimes Henry gave him permission to go on his own. At one William received so many blows to his helmet that it was beaten out of shape so that he could not get it off again. At the feast which followed the tournament one of the ladies sent a present of a large **pike** to the knight who had fought most worthily. They decided to present it to William Marshal, but when they went to look for him, they found him kneeling in the blacksmith's shop with his head on the anvil, while the blacksmith hammered away to get his helmet off. It must have been very uncomfortable and everyone felt he deserved the prize.

Here is the story of another tournament, held at Joigni (in France), as it is told in the poem about William the Marshal.

> The Marshal and his company sped so well that they arrived outside the castle of Joigni in good time and dismounted in a pleasant and delightful spot outside it. Then the Countess came forth, who was as proper as nature could **fashion** her, and with her were ladies and **damsels** so adorned and so fair that their beauty was beyond reproach, nor had they anything to learn about courtesy. The Marshal's knights sallied forth to

Knights and ladies dancing. This picture comes from a fourteenth-century book.

meet them and felt themselves the better men for the arrival of the ladies.

Then, while they waited for more knights to arrive, someone suggested: 'Let us have a dance – it will pass the time more agreeably.' So they all took hands. Then someone asked, 'Who will sing for us?' Then the Marshal, who sang well though he never boasted of anything, began a song in a sweetly-tuned voice. It greatly pleased all who were present and they joined in the chorus with a will. When his song, which had given them great pleasure and delight, was finished, a minstrel struck up another. I do not know what it was about, but the chorus ran:

Marshal, I pray,
Give me a noble horse this day!

When the Marshal heard it, he stayed no longer where he was, but quitted the dance without a word. A squire led up his horse and he beckoned to the little minstrel who ran after him as hard as his legs would carry him. Now some **jousters** were coming up for the tournament. The Marshal, without wasting time in argument, went for one of them with such confidence in his stout lance that, without more ado, he sent him flying out of the saddle. Then he made the little minstrel mount the captured horse, and he burst right into the dance, crying to everyone: 'See this horse! The Marshal has given it to me!' And everyone was amazed, for they had thought he was still dancing, and there was great talk about it.

Things to do

1. Taking hostages was a regular custom in medieval times. Write down arguments for and against it.
2. Draw a picture to illustrate one of William the Marshal's tournaments.
3. William the Marshal started as a poor knight. What helped him to get rich and important?
4. Read the story on pages 29–31 again. What does the poet mean by saying that the Countess was 'as proper as nature could fashion her' and what does he mean by 'courtesy'?

5 The story of William the Marshal (part 2)

A problem of loyalty

You will remember that a knight always took an oath of loyalty to his lord. This was very serious. When William became the young Henry's tutor he took his oath of loyalty to his young lord. But this made problems for William, because the young Henry quarrelled with his father, King Henry. Once the young Henry actually rebelled against his father, so William had to choose between two masters. What was he to do? He decided that his loyalty belonged to the young prince, so he had to support him against his father, but he did not approve of rebellion and was glad when it was over.

Then William the Marshal's service to his young lord ended suddenly and tragically when the young Henry fell ill. As he was dying, he was troubled because he had taken a vow to go on crusade and fight for the Holy Land. Now he would never be able to do it. He said to William: 'Marshal, you have always been faithful and loyal. I leave you my cross and pray you to carry it for me to the **Holy Sepulchre** at Jerusalem.' So William set out for Jerusalem, carrying Henry's cloak with the red cross on it. He was away two years, but the poem does not tell us anything about his adventures.

King Henry did not punish William for sticking to the young Henry because he valued his loyalty. So he made him one of his councillors and gave him more lands. But in two years' time the old king died and William found himself in an awkward position. Henry's second son, Richard, succeeded him as king. But only a short while before Richard, too, had been rebelling against his father. William, fighting loyally for King Henry, had attacked Richard and had actually killed his horse under him. Now William's friends said that Richard would revenge himself on the Marshal. When Richard sent for William he said: 'Marshal, the other day you wanted to kill me'. William said: 'Sire, I had no intention of killing you, nor have I ever tried to do so. I am still strong enough to direct my lance. If I had wished, I could have struck your body, but I meant only to slay your horse and I am not in the least sorry for that.' Richard said: 'Marshal, I pardon you.' He liked William's frank and courteous words and he knew what a faithful servant he had been to his father, the old Henry, and to his brother, the young Henry.

William becomes one of the chief lords of England

William became the loyal servant of King Richard who gave him one of the richest heiresses in England for a wife. She was Isabel de Clare and she owned lands in many parts of England, including two splendid castles at Chepstow on the river Wye and Pembroke in south Wales. Now William had to attend to the business of governing and defending his lands, instead of going to tournaments. When King Richard went away on a crusade to the Holy Land, William Marshal worked hard to defend the king's lands. He even had to fight Prince John, Richard's young brother, who rebelled against him when Richard was captured on his way home and thrown into prison in Germany. William worked faithfully to collect a large sum of money for Richard's ransom. When the king finally came home he greeted William as one of his most loyal men.

One more fight

Although now middle-aged, William could still fight well and climb siege ladders fast. One day, when Richard was

Besieging a castle. The artist who drew this picture for a fourteenth-century book has made the fighters too big and the castle too small. In how many ways are the enemy attacking the castle? What are the defenders doing?

besieging a castle in France, they set ladders against the castle walls and swarmed up them. But the garrison defended themselves so well that one ladder was thrown right down with all the knights on it and the besiegers were driven off the others. A knight named Guy who had reached the top of a ladder was caught round his neck by a great fork and held there. William the Marshal was standing on the edge of the moat directing the attack. He saw the knight's danger and, leaping into the moat, he climbed the opposite bank and then went up the ladder, sword in hand. He attacked those who were holding Guy so fiercely that they fled.

Then his men, seeing William in triumph on the wall, cheered loudly, crying: 'The castle is taken! To his aid!' and rushed up the ladders again. Meanwhile, the constable of the castle attacked William, but with one mighty blow William brought him down and made him prisoner. By this time William was beginning to feel a little tired. He thought he had done his bit, so he sat down calmly on his prisoner and waited until the English had finished capturing the castle. When it was over King Richard said: 'Sir Marshal, it is not fitting for a man of your rank to risk yourself in such **exploits**. Leave them to younger knights.' William was fifty-three then, but I think he enjoyed showing them that he could still go up a siege-ladder with all his armour on.

William grows old serving kings

After serving the old Henry and the young Henry and King Richard, William served King John and finally John's nine-year-old son, when he became King Henry III. He fought their battles, he guarded their castles, he gave them good **counsel** and he was always loyal. King John, as you can guess, did not like him, but he knew he could not do without this true servant. William certainly did not approve of all the things King John did, but he would not fight against him. So he would not join the barons when they forced John to make promises of good government in **Magna Carta**. But once this document had been sealed he determined to see that it was kept.

Then suddenly King John died and there was a great problem. Who should rule in the name of the little nine-year-old boy who was now king? William was seventy-two years old. Everyone said that they must choose the most true and wise baron to rule and then they all agreed that this was William the Marshal. William said he was too old and feeble and suggested Ranulf, Earl of Chester. But Ranulf said: 'No, Marshal, that cannot be. You are so good a knight, so fine a man, so feared, so loved and so wise, that you are thought to be one of the first knights in the world. I say to you in all loyalty that you must be chosen.' Once William was persuaded that this was his duty, he swore to serve the little king, Henry III, to the uttermost. He said: 'If all should abandon the king except me, I would carry him on my shoulders now here, now there, from isle to isle, from land to land and I would never fail him even if I were forced to beg my bread.'

So William the Marshal was made Regent of England. For three years he fought to defend the little king. He had to fight against a French prince who was invading England and many rebel barons. At the end of three years he had turned the invaders out, recaptured the king's castles, beaten his enemies and brought peace to the country. Then he resigned. His work was done.

The end of the story

William went to his manor of Caversham, on the river Thames, close to Reading. His faithful servant and friend, John d'Erley, was there with him and he afterwards told the end of the story to the poet who wrote the poem about William.

> On the day after he had resigned the Regency, it was the Marshal's good pleasure to summon before him all his household. 'Sires,' he said, 'God be thanked, I may well exult whether it be for life or for death, I am now quit of a heavy burden. It would be well that I should complete my last will and testament and that I should make provision for my soul, for the body is in **jeopardy** and I would do well to **disencumber** myself of all earthly things and turn my thoughts to things of heaven.' 'My lord', said his son, 'we wonder much where you wish to be buried.' Then William gave directions for his funeral and for his burial in **the Temple**. He told his son to give food, drink, clothes and shoes to a hundred poor people on the day of his funeral.
>
> One day his five daughters came in to see him. The earl was surrounded by his knights. William said: 'It is an extraordinary thing: I don't know why it is but I have a great desire to sing.' John d'Erley advised him to try – it might bring back his appetite. 'Be silent,' said William, 'it would not do me any good and everyone would think I was crazy.' Then someone

William the Marshal's tomb in the Temple Church, London.

said: 'Sire, call your daughters, that they may sing and comfort you.' So the Lady Matilda sang a verse of a song in a sweet simple voice. When Jeanne's turn came, she sang very timidly. William gently reproved her: 'Do not have a shamefaced air when you sing; that is not the way to become a good singer.' Then he showed her how to sing. When the girls had finished their father dismissed them: 'Daughters, I pray God to guard you.'

Then the Marshal sent for his retainers and the countess (his wife). To the countess he said: 'My dear love, you must kiss me now, since it will be for the last time.' He wept and she wept and all the noble retainers who were present wept also for very love. His sons and many of his household kept watch. John d'Erley said: 'My lord, what would you wish to have done with your gowns and furs?' A certain cleric, Philip, spoke up loudly: 'My lord, there are many splendid gowns of scarlet with new trimmings of grey squirrel fur, and many other furs, handsome and unworn. You could sell them to buy the absolution of your sins.' 'Be silent, wretch,' said the earl, 'your **ignoble** words trouble me deeply. Soon it will be **Whitsuntide** and I know well that my knights have a right to the gift of a gown, the last gowns they will ever receive from me. Come hither, John d'Erley, I bid you, by the faith you owe to me and to God, that you give away these gowns to my knights. If there are not enough, send to London for more.' To his son he said: 'Fair son, I beg you to say farewell in my name to all who have served me well. Thank them for good faith, and may they have thanks from Almighty God alike for their words and deeds.' So the gowns were distributed and when they were shared out, there was not a knight of his household who did not receive one.

Thus died the Marshal and since he was noble in death as in life we trust that he is among the saved with God. And so ends the story of the Earl Marshal, which ought to be loved and enjoyed in every place where it is heard.

Things to do

1. Many of William the Marshal's tournaments and fights took place in France. Find out why English kings and knights were in France in the twelfth century.
2. Tell the story of the knight Guy's adventure (page 34) as if he were telling it afterwards himself.
3. In the stories in this book ladies are important. What different parts did they play?
4. Was William right to give away all his gowns at the end to his knights instead of having them sold to buy prayers for his soul?

6 A hundred years later

Below: Two knights in plate armour, engraved in brass in a church to mark the tombs of Sir R. Swynborne and his son.

If we move on a hundred years from the time of William the Marshal, we still find knights going to tournaments and fighting in wars. Their armour is heavier and more elaborate. Their castles are grander and more comfortable. They still think of themselves as the most important part of an army in a battle, but actually they are steadily becoming less important in fighting, as you will see.

Armour for knights and horses

Look back at the picture of William the Marshal on page 37. Do you remember that his armour was chain mail, made of tiny metal rings linked together? You could move fairly easily in a hauberk made of chain mail and it protected you quite well, but sometimes arrows or a very strong sword thrust pierced right through it. So gradually knights began to put heavier armour, called **plate armour**, on top of chain mail. This was made of whole metal plates. First the knight put on his hauberk or perhaps a leather tunic and then a complete metal breast-plate which covered his chest. Then there were metal pieces to cover his shoulders and elbows, thighs and legs. These pieces of plate armour were all fastened with eyelet holes and laces to what he had on underneath. He also had metal footwear made of overlapping plates and jointed gauntlet gloves. His helmet was large, generally with a visor which pulled down over his face and slits so that he could see out.

All this plate armour was very heavy, perhaps 50 or 60 pounds in weight. The helmet alone might weigh nearly 20 pounds, especially if it had a crest on top. This was the knight's special badge to show who he was when his visor was down. It might be an animal head or a bird and was made of wood or leather boiled till it was very hard. On his shield he had his family badge and he often wore a surcoat on top with his coat of arms.

Horses, too, had pieces of armour to protect their heads and shoulders. The saddle was high and heavy to help the rider stay on and the poor horse often had to wear a large embroidered cloth as well. Horses had to be large, heavy animals, like our cart-horses, for when a knight in full armour had been helped up on to his mount the horse had a terrific weight to carry. No wonder that when a horse and its rider fell down in tournament or battle neither could get up off the ground without being lifted. Far more knights probably died from being crushed or suffocated by the weight of their armour than were actually killed by sword or lance thrust.

Sir Geoffrey Luttrell saying goodbye to his wife and daughter. What is his wife handing up to him? What is embroidered on the horse-cloth? This was the family for whom the Luttrell Psalter was made in the fourteenth century.

More comfortable castles

Do you remember how cold and draughty it was living in a twelfth-century castle keep? By the fourteenth century people were beginning to give up the old keeps. The new idea was that you had very strong walls, with many round towers along them, a moat all round outside, a **barbican** and a gatehouse specially planned to keep out attackers. You can read about these in another 'Then and There' book, *The Medieval Castle*. Because of these strong outer defences people did not need to have such a strong keep inside. Instead they built the rooms they wanted for living in round the courtyard. There would be a great hall for feasting, sometimes a second hall, rooms for the lord and his guests, a chapel, rooms for servants, kitchens, stables, storage rooms and so on. The chief rooms would have fire-places and there would be proper **latrines** as well.

You would still not have found much furniture, even in the best rooms. People still sat on benches and stools, except for the chief lords and ladies who might have carved wooden chairs. But the walls would look much lighter and brighter for they were often hung all round with large pieces of cloth like curtains. These hangings were either painted or woven with patterns in bright colours. Sometimes there were hunting scenes or stories of heroes on them. When the lord of the castle moved on to another one the hangings were taken down, rolled up and carted along with his baggage.

The Hundred Years War

In the middle of the fourteenth century a great war began between England and France which lasted off and on for a hundred years. It started when the English king, Edward III, claimed that he had a right, through his mother, to be king of France. This gave English lords and knights a splendid chance to fight in what they believed was a rightful war. So, led by Edward III and later by his son who was called the Black Prince, they packed themselves, their armour and horses into the small ships of the time and crossed the Channel. Then they rode into the French country, burning crops and destroying houses as they went.

We know a lot about the first part of this war because a Frenchman, named Jean Froissart, wrote a chronicle about it. Later he came to England and presented his book to the king. He was not really on either the French or the English side. He just loved any knights in armour riding out to battle with their gold and blue and red banners waving. He wrote: 'It was a beauty to behold the banners and the **pennons** shining against the sun.' You would never think from this that fighting was a terrible, ugly thing of blood and smashed-up bodies.

Froissart's stories

What Froissart most admired were gallant knights doing brave deeds on their own. Here is one of his stories. Some English knights were shut up in a castle besieged by the French who had a powerful catapult which kept sending large stones crashing into the castle. An English knight, Sir Walter Manny, got his friends together. They dashed out, quickly destroyed the catapult and then wheeled round to get back to the castle before they were caught. But the French came galloping after them like madmen. Then Sir Walter said: 'May my lady never love me if I do not fight these men!' So they turned round and fought gallantly until the enemy drew back. When they returned to the castle the lady of the castle came down to welcome them and kissed them for their brave deeds.

There were two famous battles in the war, at places called Crecy and Poitiers. Froissart tells us a story about the battle of Poitiers when the Black Prince was in command. One of his friends said to him: 'I have taken a vow to be first into the battle.' The Prince replied: 'Sir James, may God grant you strength this day to be the most valorous of all my knights.' So Sir James and his four squires were allowed to ride out ahead of the whole army.

He fought a fierce duel with one of the French leaders who was captured in the end.

Did knights win battles?

Froissart tells us more about knights in battle than about other sorts of soldiers. But the English also had strong bands of archers with longbows who could fire a deadly rain of arrows at an advancing enemy. When the proud French knights came galloping on with all their brilliant banners flying, this hail of arrows took them by surprise.

In this battle scene from a fifteenth-century book archers with longbows seem to be doing more damage than the knights on horseback.

Even if their armour protected them, their poor horses were struck. They reared and bolted, or fell on top of their riders. The whole battle turned into confusion; a horrible mix-up of horses and men piled up on the ground. Then the English knights who had been dismounted behind the archers could rush forward to finish the battle. That was how the English won the battles of Crecy and Poitiers. The knights looked splendid, but they were no longer as much use in fighting a battle as archers who were just ordinary soldiers trained to shoot their arrows with deadly aim.

Knights of the Garter

King Edward and his lords, however, still believed that the noblest way of fighting was by knights doing brave deeds. They told stories about the famous King Arthur who sent his knights out to find great adventures and feasted them at his Round Table when they came back. So King Edward thought he would like to copy King Arthur. In 1344 at his castle of Windsor he started a company of knights called the Knights of the Garter. Like Arthur's knights they were to come back once a year to hold a feast and to worship God in a special chapel at Windsor. This was named after St George, because they thought that St George had been a brave knight who rescued people from a terrible dragon. There were twenty-six Knights of the Garter to begin with. The queen still has Knights of the Garter and once a year they go in procession to St George's chapel. If you visit it you will see that each knight has a special seat with his banner hanging above it.

A perfect knight

The poet Geoffrey Chaucer was living in London at this time. He must have seen many knights riding through the streets and listened to their stories of adventure. In his *Canterbury Tales* – which were about a company of pilgrims telling stories as they rode to Canterbury – he describes a very good knight. He tells us that this knight had loved chivalry, truth and honour, freedom and courtesy since the very first days when he began to ride. He had adventured in many strange lands and had fought the enemies of Christians in far-off places. But although he had done such brave deeds, he was modest and mild, never bragging about himself and never saying anything rude about anyone. He was a really perfect, gentle knight, Chaucer says, although his clothes were very plain and much worn, for he had only just come back from his travels.

Chaucer liked to think that there were noble knights like

The knight (right) and squire (left) in the Canterbury Tales drawn near the time of Chaucer. Does the knight look like Chaucer's description on this page? The squire was embroidered like a meadow full of flowers and knew how to sit a horse and ride.

this, but most of the real knights were not very noble. They were greedy to snatch at **loot** – horses, armour, rich robes, gold and silver – when they fought in a war and one of their aims was to capture rich prisoners who could be exchanged for large ransoms. They treated noble prisoners courteously and were quite fair to each other, but they were often terribly cruel to poor peasants and townspeople. Once the Black Prince was very angry with the bishop of a French town called Limoges. He said that the bishop had been a traitor to him. But instead of trying to punish the bishop, the Black Prince ordered that all the people in Limoges, women and children as well as men, were to be butchered. The slaughter was terrible, as the English soldiers rode through the masses of people all begging for their lives. It was a horrible thing to do and yet the Black Prince was supposed to be a model knight.

A great tournament

In the year 1390 the grandson of Edward III, King Richard II, announced a grand tournament to be held in London. No one thought that the time was past for such shows, for people still loved to dress up in their armour and ride out with banners flying. This is how Froissart describes the occasion:

> The king ordered grand tournaments and feasts to be held in London, where sixty knights were to come, accompanied by sixty most noble ladies richly ornamented and dressed. They were to go in procession from the Tower of London with their ladies and parade through the streets to a large open field called Smithfield. There they were to wait the arrival of any foreign knights who might come to joust. The prize for the best knight on the foreign side was to be a rich crown of gold and for the most gallant home knight, a very rich golden clasp.
>
> So on the Sunday afternoon there paraded from the Tower of London sixty splendid horses ornamented for

the tournament, and on each was mounted a squire of honour. Then rode sixty noble ladies most elegantly and richly dressed, each leading a knight with a silver chain, completely armed for **tilting**. And they were attended by many trumpets and minstrels.

When the tournament began everyone fought as hard as possible, many were unhorsed and many more lost their helmets. The jousting continued with great courage until night put an end to it. The prizes were given at suppertime. On the next day the squires tilted and after supper the dancing lasted until daybreak. The rest of the week was spent in feasting.

There is much to see in this fifteenth-century picture of a tournament. What is happening at this very moment? What is the king going to do? Why are the trumpets blowing? Can you find the man who is probably the umpire?

Great changes

That was not the last big tournament. Knights went on pretending that they could win battles with swords and lances and so they must have tournaments for practice. But soon battles were going to be won, not even by archers, but by big guns. You cannot fight a cannon by charging it on horseback with your lance. Big changes were coming in, but people did not want to see them. So even a hundred years after that tournament at Smithfield, William Caxton, who printed some of our first English books, was telling the knights of his day not to be lazy but to get up and learn to fight on horseback. 'O ye knights of England,' he said 'what do you do now but go to the baths and play at dice? Look back to the time when there were many knights in England who knew their horses and their horses knew them! I wish our sovereign king would announce jousts of peace two or three times a year, so that every knight would be ready with his horse and his armour and would practise the skill of a knight. Then gentlemen would follow the ancient custom of chivalry and be always ready to serve their king.'

How surprised Caxton would have been if he could have seen the way modern wars are fought!

Things to do

1. Draw a knight in plate armour.
2. Find out more about the battles of Crecy and Poitiers and the part the archers played in them.
3. Get a book about Chaucer's *Canterbury Tales* from the library and read about the other pilgrims besides the knight.

How do we know?

What we can see with our eyes

Castles There are many castles scattered round Britain, some ruined, some with later buildings added on. When you visit a castle, try to pick out the different parts of it (e.g. gatehouse, keep, courtyard, great hall, etc.) and remind yourself of what medieval knights did there.

In museums Many museums have suits of armour and weapons such as swords and lances. Study these carefully and imagine what it would be like to fight with this armour and weapons. Decide whether the particular examples of armour that you see are chain mail, plate armour, or a bit of both.

In churches Many churches have splendid tombs of knights in armour, often with their pet dogs at their feet. There are sometimes brass figures of knights on the floor and in a few places knights are carved on the underside of tip-up wooden seats in the church **chancel**.

Pictures of knights which monks drew in the margins of their books. Sometimes they are fighting, sometimes riding at the quintain or tilting in tournaments, sometimes feasting, hunting or playing games.

What we read in chronicles, poems and stories

Chroniclers loved writing about fighting and brave deeds. So they give us many descriptions of battles and of besieging castles. Froissart is one of the best of these. Then there are long story poems about knights. These often began as songs sung by troubadours to entertain people at feasts. Then they got written down. You will have read in this book several stories which come from these poems. In particular, the whole story of William the Marshal comes from a long French poem called Guillaume le Maréchal. These chronicles and poems are mostly in Latin or old French but I have translated them here. Chaucer's *Canterbury Tales* are in what is called middle English but they have been translated many times. The stories of King Arthur were written down by various people and finally put together by a knight named Sir Thomas Malory who lived not long before Caxton.

Things to do in a group

1. Read 'A knight's excuses for fighting' (page 12). Discuss whether you think they are good reasons. War always kills or hurts many innocent people (like the people of Limoges, page 46). Are there any good reasons for going to war?
2. Discuss what you think 'loyalty' means. Was William the Marshal loyal to the right people?
3. Changes are always happening in history. Discuss what great changes have happened in the last fifty years. Do we hang on to old ways of doing things too long?
4. Make a book or a set of pictures showing different kinds of armour and how it changed. If there is a church near you with figures of knights in it, you could draw them for your book, or if they are brass figures you might find out how to do 'brass rubbings'.
5. Make a set of pictures to show the story of William the Marshal *or* make up a play about some of the adventures he had.
6. Make a model of a tournament with cardboard figures and horses.
7. If you live near enough, visit St George's chapel at Windsor and make drawings of some of the coats of arms belonging to present Knights of the Garter.

Glossary

archery	shooting with a bow and arrows
armourer	man who makes and looks after **armour**
armoury	room in a castle where armour was stored
bailey	castle yard with wall, bank or moat, or all three round it
ballad	long story poem, often sung to an audience
barbican	fortifications outside a castle gatehouse
battlements	low wall and walk round the top of a castle wall
beleaguered	besieged
boar	wild pig
butt	target for shooting arrows at
chain mail	armour made of linked rings of metal
chancel	the part of the church with the altar and seats for the choir
chausses	armour covering the legs
chivalry	rules of good behaviour for a knight who is **chivalrous** when he keeps them
coat of arms	the special badge of a family painted on a shield
conical	shaped like a cone
contemporary	here means something written at the same time as the events described
counsel	advice
courteous	being polite
courtesy	good manners, politeness
crusader	knight who went to fight for the Church in what was thought to be a holy war
damsel	young girl
to **disemcumber**	to get rid of
to **divert**	here means to amuse
exploit	a deed of bravery or daring
falconer	man who looks after **falcons**, a kind of hawk
to **fashion**	here means to make
favour	here means a gift from a lady to a knight
fletcher	man who makes arrows
gambeson	padded leather tunic
to **garrison**	to keep soldiers in a castle in order to protect it from attack
hauberk	tunic of chain mail
Holy Sepulchre	the tomb of Christ in Jerusalem
honour	here means all the lands, manors and castles owned by one lord

hostage someone taken prisoner in order to force someone else to do something or to keep a promise
ignoble mean, unworthy
jeopardy danger
jouster knight who takes part in **jousting**, that is, sham fighting
keep chief and strongest tower in a castle
lance spear
latrine very simple kind of toilet or lavatory
loot things captured from an enemy in war
Magna Carta the Great Charter, a list of promises made by King John to his barons
mangonel large catapult for attacking castles
oath of fealty solemn promise made to a lord to serve him faithfully
palfrey small horse
pavillion here means a large tent
pennon small flag
pewter mixture of tin and copper used to make plates and mugs
pike here means a large fish
plantain common plant with a long stem and a head
plate armour armour made of solid metal plates
quarry here means a hunted animal or bird
quintain a stand used by knights for practising fighting with a lance
ransom money paid to set a prisoner free
to **reprieve** to pardon
sconce holder fixed to the wall to hold a torch or candle
shaft handle
solar private room in a castle for the lord or lady
steward man who manages the lord's affairs
surcoat tunic worn over armour, often with the family coat of arms on it
tankard metal mug
to **tilt** to practise fighting on horseback with a lance
tilting yard place for tilting
the Temple a church in London where many knights were buried
tournament competitions in sham fighting on horse and on foot
troubadour poet who sang songs about love and war to knights and ladies
truce when enemies agree to stop fighting for a certain time
vassal knight who has sworn to serve a lord in return for land
vestments special robes worn by priests
visor part of a helmet covering the face which can be lifted to see out
Whitsuntide the Christian festival of Pentecost which comes seven weeks after Easter

Index